D0934755

THE TOP PERFORMER'S GUIDE TO LEADERSHIP

ESSENTIAL SKILLS THAT PUT YOU ON TOP

JUDITH ORLOFF, MEd

SOURCEBOOKS, INC.
NAPERVILLE, ILLINOIS

8-21-8

Published by Sourcebooks, Inc.
P.O. Box 4410, Naperville, Illinois 60567-4410
(630) 961-3900
Fax: (630) 961-2168
www.sourcebooks.com

Orloff, Judith.
  The top performer's guide to leadership / by Judith Orloff.
     p. cm.
  Includes index.
  ISBN 978-1-4022-0964-2 (hbk.)
  1. Leadership. I. Title.

HD57.7.O75 2008
658.4'092--dc22

                              2007039524

Printed and bound in United States of America.
BG 10 9 8 7 6 5 4 3 2 1

DEDICATION

Extraordinary results are achieved by Top Performance Teams, as well as by individuals. This book is dedicated to my colleagues and client partners from superb companies such as Bank of America, Fleet Bank, Wellbridge, Midas International, Lubuvitz of Bucks County, and others, and to all my associates from all over the world and through the years. I am grateful to my family and friends for their encouragement and laughter while writing this book. I particularly wish to thank my son Adam Fels, who looked over all my ideas and added wonderful insights from the world of learning, from his role as principal of a middle school in Louisville, Colorado; and my husband Jonathan Falk for his unending willingness to listen to rewrites and my fears about "getting it right." I am also grateful to my business partner and friend of twenty-five years, Sarah Cardet.

CONTENTS

INTRODUCTION

This book is about creating Top Performance Leadership. It is intended to help you become a Top Performance Leader, a person achieving extraordinary results while partnering with peers, teams, managers, and direct reports. What is a Top Performance Leader? And who are they? What are the qualities, values, and competencies distinguishing them from other leaders? Peter Senge, a leadership guru and author of *Synchronicity: The Inner Path of Leadership*, said, "Leadership is about creating a domain in which human beings continually deepen their understanding of reality and become more capable of participating in the unfolding world. Ultimately, leadership is about creating new realities."

While a psychotherapist in Vermont, it was my good fortune to meet Marshall Thurber, the creator of the seminar "Money and You." It was a transforming experience. I discovered aspects of my personality not previously obvious to me. They had been in "shadow," meaning I couldn't see them very clearly. Now I understand many of the judgments I had about other people

---

Senge, P, 1990, "Introduction to Synchronicity." In *Synchronicity: the Inner Path of Leadership*, Jaworski, J, San Francisco, Berrett Koehler. This is the heart of the journey for the Top Performance Leader.

were really about me and my mental makeup. Before this self-discovery, I was often disappointed in my relationships. I also didn't understand that much of what I admired or envied in others was available to me, if only I shifted my perception to include all of who I am. As I left this three-day seminar, I decided to learn more about this "shadow" so I could "see the light." My journey is still in progress and this book is a testimony to the miles recorded.

My first step in becoming a Top Performance Leader was following my vision to share the insights I had gained. I left my therapy practice in Burlington, Vermont, to facilitate one of Marshall's seminars called "Secrets of a Powerful Presentation." This was a six-day workshop designed to help people resolve their past traumas so they could live fruitful, powerful lives. Many business leaders signed up for this program right out of the "Money and You" seminar.

In 1983, my first year of facilitating these seminars, most of the participants were men. They were strongly committed to success. Though they were traditional in their politics, outlook on marriage, and social issues, they were willing to open up their hearts and minds to me, a woman. I was privileged to facilitate this workshop for a few years in America, Australia, and New Zealand. Many of the participants continued to learn with me, signing up for a year-long program to examine their questions about leadership, integrity, responsibility, conflict, change, and team building.

Thereafter, I moved to San Diego and cofounded Choices International, a personal growth company designed to support successful entrepreneurs. This led to the formation of Educational Discoveries. The mantra at Educational Discoveries was personal growth, leadership development, and business savvy.

We rapidly matured into a successful training and development company working with multinational organizations such as Bank of America, ABB, Caterpillar, and Cargill. Everyone we hired—from receptionist to COO—was supported to become a Top Performance Leader. Although Top Performance Leaders are unusual in the general business environment, they became the norm in our company. Our environment was designed for Top Performance.

Once in a very great while, an employee or client surfaced as a Top Performance Leader, no matter what their designated role. They naturally created an environment of leadership and empowered others to do the same. Much of what I learned from growing Educational Discoveries and from working with our clients is reflected in this book.

There are eight key areas of development important for Top Performance Leadership.

- Awareness, Beliefs, and Values
- Integrity and Responsibility
- Vision and Action
- Listening and Communicating
- Intention, Motivation, and Influence
- Thriving in Paradox
- Conflict: Your Ally and Coach
- Empowerment and Synergy

Following is a brief summary of each area of development. Each area will be explained in more detail in subsequent chapters.

Awareness, Beliefs, and Values
Creating our experience of reality

As infants and young children, we are aware of the world around us in a pure form. We simply experience what is. As we get older, we learn to adapt so that we fit into our family. Most of the time, we "follow the leader"—either our parents or older siblings. As we move out into the world, our awareness opens to new heights, at times coinciding with our family, while at other times being in conflict with our familiar world. Our degree of self-awareness allows us more or less freedom in our choices.

Typically, as children, many of our major decisions are made for the purpose of survival. We seek to make sense of the world around us and reach an acceptable level of comfort and safety. Over time, our beliefs, formed as a response to our family values, begin to create our world: first, we believe what we see, and then we see what we believe. In Chapter 1, you will sharpen your awareness, identify the beliefs that affect your performance, and learn to become aware of the pattern of movement that supports the attainment of your vision. This understanding, commitment, and willingness to observe your beliefs and behaviors is profound. As you learn to listen to your inner awareness and personal truth, you will experience greater personal effectiveness and peace of mind.

Integrity and Responsibility
Integrity: Being whole and complete
When a person is in a state of integrity, he or she appears to be like an alchemist: what he or she touches turns to gold, that is, success. Life seems easy. When decisions and actions are congruent with their values, these people experience undiminished energy and replenished inner resources.

Integrity is always obvious to those who have a fair share of it themselves. Top Performance Leaders, as defined in this book, are models of integrity. In Chapter 2, you will learn how to trust and be at ease with difficult decisions. You will be able to sleep at night!

Responsibility: Unlimited Possibilities

Responsibility connects you to your creative force. To some, the word "responsibility" may connote doing the right thing or bearing the burden of obligation. In the context of Top Performance Leadership, to be personally responsible means "response-ability."

Response-ability helps to align every aspect of the business to the vision. You will find that response-able actions create an irresistible magnetism for the resources, people, and events necessary to the accomplishment of goals.

Top Performance Leaders are not bound by the past or seduced by the future. They know that although the legacy, history, and vision of the company are crucial aspects of an elegant strategy for the future, they can count on their commitment, knowledge, and personal integrity to make the correct decisions at the correct time.

Vision and Action

The ability to create a clear and powerful vision of a desired outcome is an indispensable element of success for the Top Performance Leader. The vision, coupled with a clear knowledge of current reality, enables a leader to identify the actions that will lead to desired results. In this chapter, you will examine your purpose and vision, making sure it aligns with the vision of your organization. If it doesn't, we will offer ways that it can. You will learn how to *embody* this shared vision. You will also foresee the potential obstacles to achieve this vision and discover ideas for removing them.

Listening and Communicating

Communication theory asserts that words are at most 10 percent of a communication. Yet, many people respond to that 10 percent and are baffled when there is a misinterpretation. Negotiations and conflict resolution that result from understanding what is being "said" underneath the words, including defenses and hidden agendas, are extremely powerful and effective. By tuning in to *meaning* rather than words, you can avert crisis, remove obstacles, and create Top Performance. Chapter 4 will also show you how to generate authentic connections that will allow you to become a trusted advisor.

The art of powerful communication is not difficult to master, nor is it some kind of magical skill that only a lucky few possess. A Top Performance Leader communicates vision, ideas, and intended results with power, clarity, and simplicity. When the leader can communicate his meaning through the words he speaks and is able to hear the meaning in another person's words, the result is connection and understanding. He or she is "in sync" with the people around him. For Top Performance Leaders, all conversations are meaningful, and transferring knowledge and confidence with each word they speak is an ordinary part of their workday.

Intention, Motivation, and Influence

Many of us find it difficult to inspire peers and team members to be truly powerful, personally responsible, and genuinely self-starting. Learning to become aware of other's intentions and dreams is a skill needed to achieve the desired results. Top Performance Leaders motivate and influence by demonstration, empathy, and dialogue. The "rah, rah, sis boom bah" of the past is no longer relevant. In this chapter you will learn to naturally inspire others to be their best and get results. You will also learn how to create a team that is self-aware, self-starting, self-motivating, and self-influencing.

Thriving in Paradox

We live in a time of unprecedented, ever-present, and accelerating change. The core skill of masters in leading change is the ability to deal with paradox. You will be able to handle many seemingly contradictory behaviors, ideas, or situations at the same time. Developing this ability is part of the process of moving from being individual contributors to leading a team or leading the company.

The dilemma is: how to take care of business? The answer is to keep operations going evenly from day to day and, at the same time, innovate and take risks. Alone, neither will create success. In Chapter 5 you will learn how to identify and enjoy paradox. You will learn how to include all your experiences, no matter how chaotic, while maintaining the ability to decide when and how to take action.

Conflict: Your Ally and Coach

How we respond to conflicts—internally and externally —is our own choice. The Top Performance Leader learns to acknowledge what is really going on. He or she gains the advantage of a clear choice and the ability to respond to conflict creatively rather than as a reaction to the past. Stress and anxiety are not a part of the process.

In Chapter5 you will see how conflict is an opportunity to grow and is not cause for stress. You will be able to resolve intense, real-life business or personal conflict situations and learn how internal stress can be transformed into motivation. Stress is a constant and is an aspect of every process. It is neutral and need not be experienced as negative.

Empowerment and Synergy: Giving Away Power Builds More

Many leaders believe empowerment means giving authority and increasing another's self-esteem. This misunderstanding of empowerment has created organizational crises and chaos. A Top Performance Leader understands that empowerment occurs when the other person truly "gets" what you are passing on to him or her—both the content and the context. How you pass on skills and knowledge is as important as the skills and knowledge. Here we will talk about how to transmit your point of view while giving another the authority to make decisions that affect your life.

The whole is greater than the sum of the parts

Occasionally, we learn of a group or team that surpasses its individual capabilities and, through the power of its collective energy, creates results that far exceed expectations. The young, inexperienced U.S. Hockey Team stunned the world in 1980 by winning the Olympic gold medal from vastly more talented and experienced Russian and Finnish teams. The key to that kind of performance in sports, business, and human affairs is synergy—the whole being greater than the sum of its parts.

Many leaders are unable to shift from their comfort zone; they prefer a familiar mode of doing and performing. In Chapter 6 you will experience what synergy is, and learn how to create it in all business and personal situations.

Top Performance Leadership
Self-assessment

Please take a moment to answer the following questions as honestly as possible. You'll be asked to repeat this exercise at the end of the book. As you go through the exercises in each chapter, take a minute to look at these answers and note how you feel.

1. Why did you choose the work that you do?

   _____

   _____

   _____

2. You can convince the world of the value of one particular thing, the thing that you have spent your life learning. What is it?

   _____

   _____

   _____

3. You can reach others in a way that touches them enough to change the way they work in the world. What is the way?

   _____

   _____

   _____

4. You will leave your children or others' children the legacy of one piece of wisdom to make their lives successful. What is that piece of wisdom?

   _____

   _____

   _____

5. Synergy lights up a group of people so that they act as a single entity. How do you describe "synergy"?

_____

_____

_____

6. Describe your relationships with your peers, coworkers, manager, and leadership team.

_____

_____

_____

7. What inspires you at work?

_____

_____

_____

8. What do you want to change or discard at work?

_____

_____

_____

9. A. What are your dreams, hopes, goals for the next few years?

_____

_____

_____

B. What are your dreams, hopes, goals for the future?

_____

_____

_____

10. What do you want to accomplish in your life overall? What do you want your life to mean? (Please answer one of these.)

_____

_____

_____

11. Look at your answer to question 10. What challenges do you have to overcome to accomplish this?

_____

_____

_____

12. What are some of your major fears?

_____

_____

_____

13. What upsets are you currently experiencing at work?

_____

_____

_____

14. What is your most negative thought about yourself?

_____

_____

_____

15. What is your most positive thought about yourself?

_____

_____

_____

16. On a scale of one to ten, with ten being the top, rate how well you:
    • Share your truth _____
    • Accept feedback _____
    • Take risks _____
    • Ask for help _____
    • Change your point of view _____
    • Communicate _____
    • Show love _____
    • Receive love _____
    • Behave responsibly _____
    • Tolerate paradox _____
    • Forgive _____

17. What communication skills do you want to strengthen?

_____

_____

_____

18. What interpersonal skills do you want to strengthen?

_____

_____

_____

19. Do you have a spiritual practice? If so, please describe.

_____

_____

_____

20. When you feel resistance to making a change, how does that resistance reveal itself to you? How do you show it externally?

_____

_____

_____

CHAPTER 1

SELF-AWARENESS

"What is necessary to change a person is to change his awareness of himself."
—*Abraham Maslow (American philosopher and psychologist, 1908–1970)*

When Educational Discoveries was at its peak, we had approximately 110 employees including independent contractors. We had a wonderful workspace, including a kitchen and great coffee, and we had a solid set of operating principles that we asked everyone to agree to. These agreements were discussed at every job interview and were used as a barometer to determine whether or not the applicant would fit in our culture. Most people easily agreed to keep them, and in fact, applauded us for our positive attitude. In our new employee trainings we did our best to ensure that the new employees understood what was being asked of them. They could also attend practice sessions demonstrating the agreements. The following are some of these operating agreements.

Operating Agreements

Assume positive intent—Respond to others' behavior as if they are doing what they believe is right. Do your best to not see their behavior as personal to you; instead, recognize it as the way they are with everyone. This is a life-long process. Keeping this agreement requires you to become aware of your own intentions and beliefs.

Know yourself—This entails giving up blame, projection, and judgment. It also means not trying to be a hero and "fix" others. By attempting to fix people we see them as broken, and we may disrespect their freedom to choose their own life by interfering.

Give and receive feedback—Share your experience without judging and ask the same from others. This includes not justifying, explaining, or defending yourself when you receive feedback. It is important to take time to consider feedback. Contemplating on its meaning will help you to realize its true worth.

Be personally responsible—Be aware that you are accountable for your experience and interpretation of an event .This will help you avoid blame or excuses for your behavior. It will open up possibilities for new responses to old problems.

View yourself and others as equals—No matter what a person's age, position, or perspective, everyone needs to be treated with the same respect. There is an old adage I heard from my father: "You can always tell who a person is by how he or she treats a waiter in a restaurant."

Ask for help—Mistakes are opportunities to learn. Asking for help allows for synergy and connection. Can you ask for help without feeling "less than"?

Resolve issues within forty-eight hours—Misinterpretations or differences in a point of view account for many conflicts. By resolving these conflicts quickly, you can be more productive.

A few employees decided to resign when they realized we were asking them to change their behavior. Others felt so good during the practice sessions, they became "converts" to our code of behavior.

Taking Back Your Power

In light of my work in individual and family therapy as well as in leadership development and emotional literacy, I recognize that everyone has positive and negative personality traits. My work with clients supports them to embrace their positive and negative emotions and thoughts, while doing their best to choose behaviors that serve the greater good. Successful, sustainable leadership includes the whole person with warts and imperfections.

Webster's dictionary defines *shadow* as "the dark part of a picture, representing the absence of illumination; a period or instance of gloom, unhappiness, mistrust, doubt, dissension, and the like." It also defines shadow as an inseparable companion. In other words, the shadow of the self cannot be seen, yet is with us all the time. Because these shadow personality traits are hidden, we are likely to attribute them to other people. It is always easy to present evidence that points to someone else. This goes both ways, positive and negative. If you do not accept the aspects of yourself you don't like, or if you minimize your positive qualities, you adversely affect your performance as a leader and sap your power. The following exercise can illuminate your shadow aspects.

Can you name what you are afraid of in other people? Do you know why you are afraid?

_____

_____

_____

What do you judge about others? Do you think they are manipulative, angry, covert, etc.?

_____

_____

_____

What do you admire about a person that makes you think they are smarter or nicer or better than you?

_____

_____

_____

What angers you most about your parents? Friends? Coworkers? Managers?

_____

_____

_____

What do you judge or dislike about yourself?

_____

_____

_____

Your answers to these few questions actually can tell you about those aspects of yourself that you don't like. Even though you may be factually correct in your assessment of others, the meaning and emotions you bring into consideration are usually unwarranted when based on a particular incident. Each one of us is unique, and many factors intersect to create our response in any given moment. Much of the time, we attribute the undesirable aspects of ourselves, our "shadow selves" on other people. A simple example of this is blaming another person for how we feel about him or her. This continues until we embrace all of who we are.

Projection

There are many forms of shadow. Projection is the simplest of all of them. Projection is a container that holds all the parts of ourselves we don't like or are afraid to manifest and gives them away. Of course, we don't really give them away. Most of us continue to be perplexed as to how negative situations we encounter seem to repeat themselves. We can't really get rid of our dark or shadow side. It would be like attempting to cut ourselves in half and only care for the half we like.

Understanding projection is a powerful way of gaining insight into our shadows. It works just like a movie with you as the person in the little projector room at the back of the theater. In effect, projection lends a shine to our unappreciated and emotionally discarded traits and puts them on other people's screens. The traits can be positive or negative, it doesn't matter. When it is in full play, projection dilutes our passions, and it is one of the principal obstacles stopping a Top Performance Leader from fulfilling his or her purpose.

As children, we all learned how to habitually deny truths about ourselves. This denial was not intrinsic to our nature, but learned. Remember when you were a child, and you were caught doing something you were not supposed to be doing? Many times, rather than admit that we were responsible for what occurred, we blamed others. We wanted the safety of being "good."

Over time, we convinced ourselves someone else was the cause of the situation. This denial became so ingrained that most of us don't even remember how it began. In fact, if we ask ourselves now, "What are we denying in this situation?" many times we answer with, "nothing." If we don't get the promotion we wanted, and are asked,"How do you feel about this?" We tend to answer with, "We are fine; we just haven't had the right opportunity to get ahead." If we were not in denial we might say, " I feel awful. I missed that opportunity for the promotion by not performing the best I could."

In truth, this recurrent denial saps us of our self-confidence and can eventually bring us to a standstill or a crisis. After years of firm denial, we cannot even see who we really are and our self-justification becomes an intrinsic part of our identity.

As we grow up, we continue to project our negative feelings and thoughts. We begin to believe our thoughts, feelings, and experiences come from outside. We feel victimized. As we gain emotional and social intelligence, we become aware of these blind spots in ourselves. It doesn't feel so good when we are in the middle of this discovery. It takes vigilant awareness and practice to accept this discovery.

As our awareness grows, we notice our experience of events comes from our perspective. This is difficult to get our hands around; it sure looks like others' behavior can cause our responses. So, although we know about personal responsibility and agree that we are the ones in charge, it is difficult to accept and experience it 100 percent. We are fortunate when our mistakes and personal crises lead us to direct understanding of our personal power and change how we think.

Although we can't control most situations we encounter, we can always choose our responses. We are rarely at the mercy of another person; we are always accountable to ourselves. Unfortunately, sometimes, it is easier to feel victimized rather than see ourselves as the direct cause of our responses. Top Performance Leadership and victimization are anathema to each other. It is difficult to view yourself as a victim and a Top Performance Leader at the same time.

Although it sometimes seems easier to continue to feel victimized, just think about the power you have when you realize you *can always choose your response*, in every situation without exception.

As we rescue and gather our projections from all those around us, we may experience unfamiliar truths about ourselves. Although we feel uncomfortable, if we are committed to raising our awareness, we can use our judgments about others as boomerangs, bringing us back to reflect on ourselves.

All our interpretations of our experiences in life outside of us are projections of our selves.

Projection takes a number of forms. For example, all prejudice is based on a set of beliefs rather than on reality. A prejudiced person may be unable to see who the object of his or her prejudice *really* is, and will usually prevent favorable information about that person or group of people from coming to light. Similarly, beliefs about the power given to a "boss" or a customer make it difficult to assess these relationships effectively.

Projection is an internal experience that is not conscious. By that I mean it is a relationship with the self that is played out with other people. It can manifest itself as a way of looking up to someone and seeing him or her as impervious to faults, or as seeing another as a victim or an abuser. These distinctions can arise simply by the level of agreement or disagreement that comes from the other person. Projection is part of the human condition and we can use it as a way to learn about ourselves and how we view ourselves and the world. By doing this, our performance will naturally improve and our ability to lead will be more effective.

Judgments

When we judge, we handicap our performance, as our judgments create walls and false conclusions that end reasonable inquiry. When we judge, we can't connect, and are isolated. This is true even when we are right about facts. On the other hand, when we can neutrally witness ourselves and others and provide honest feedback, we are able to perform our jobs with a high level of competence.

The lack of negative judgment can lead to new paradigms and opportunities. One of my first jobs was at Revlon, Inc. I was nineteen. I had just moved to New York City and was able to land a position at Revlon in the eye makeup department. I worked for a woman. In fact, many of the top positions at Revlon were held by women. It became natural for me to be an executive in all my jobs as I did not hold a negative judgment about a woman being in a top performing position. In fact, I held a positive attitude and expected that I would be in charge, and I assumed that role wherever I worked. If I had begun my career with a male executive as my boss, and assumed that men were leaders, not women, I may not have had the foresight to be a leader in my chosen field.

Of course, evaluation and assessment are necessary for Top Performance Leadership. Evaluation of a project, a person's performance, and the final results in the achievement of goals and strategies, are all very important. However, this kind of evaluation is based on objective criteria and falls outside the realm of judgment that targets a person's character, skin color, or sexual preference. Remember, character judgment of another person is a fear-based emotional response and does not bring out what is essentially true about that person.

Sally Van Wagenen Keil is the author of an article called, "Acting out the Family on the Job." She interviewed Harry Levinson, a psychologist at Harvard Medical School and president of the Levinson Institute. He states, "Our childhood bonds affect everything from corporate leadership to departmental feuds. . . . These emotional attachments are the key to the survival of

American business." He spoke about AT&T when they were going through their divestiture. Many people chose to work at AT&T because of its "mothering" qualities. When they were informed they could no longer maintain their roles in the new company, they were upset. AT&T was very sensitive to the situation. They realized that the company had changed, but the emotional needs of the employees had not.

Our company was hired by an ex-director to create and design a call center leadership program based on his patents and years of work with call centers. He had been with AT&T for over thirty years and was quite angry at the change they went through and how it affected him. He was unwilling to accept the change neutrally and judged and blamed them harshly for his situation. We spent an extraordinary amount of time attempting to give him what he asked for. It was impossible to please him, although our work was excellent. We eventually gave up, realizing that nothing except his going back to his paternalistic role in AT&T would satisfy. We discovered later he became embroiled in a lawsuit with AT&T accusing the leadership in the organization of personal issues. That caused the company to let him go. To this day, he is willing to spend his time in this damaging way rather than move forward. He felt that he was victimized and refuses to see it any differently.

What was the last situation or person you judged when at work or home?

_____

_____

_____

Who did you judge? What was the judgment?

_____

_____

_____

How did you handle it?

_____

_____

_____

What results did you achieve? Were you satisfied with your results?

_____

_____

_____

Did you experience yourself behaving as a Top Performance Leader?

_____

_____

_____

I remember a project we did for a large manufacturing company. We were asked to design an intervention for their purchasing department. They did not feel respected by the rest of the organization and wanted to centralize rather than be part of other departments. They believed they needed to be a separate department to retain respect. There was disagreement and dissension regarding this in the rest of the company. When we went in to perform our initial assessment, we realized they were correct in their belief that they were being judged. When we presented the results of our assessment to the leadership, we were surprised by the depth of the anger and resentment they expressed. It had permeated their belief in themselves and in fact, they were not performing with excellence. After they understood how this was affecting their performance, they were able to self-correct and recover their pride and integrity through being more responsible for how they behaved in the face of judgment. Also, they were able to keep their department centralized.

Judgment is insidious in that it has many disguises and can take hold when we are completely unaware. I remember once going to eat lunch in my company lunchroom and overhearing a conversation. The employees were discussing vacations. As I approached the cafeteria, one of them said, "Judith will only reconsider the vacation policy when she is willing to take one herself. She is really selfish." The employee was right on the money. I was stingy with vacations and thought the HR department was giving too much to people. Yet, it was my own judgment and fear of not working hard enough that didn't allow me to take vacations. I evaluated other's performance based on my own fear of failure. So I thought others didn't work hard enough. In other words, I was projecting my own fear of failure on everyone else. What an attitude! That became my experience of "selfish." Of course, the policies relating to vacation and holidays changed dramatically after that "aha" moment. Because of my judgment of taking time for myself for recreation, I was taking that joy away from everyone. What I didn't realize until that incident was that a vacation and rest allowed people to return to their work invigorated, energized, and ready to achieve new goals and aspirations.

Interpretation

Interpretation is a rational explanation of what we hear and see that helps us make sense of our experiences. However, we filter this through our emotional history and our point of view. Can our interpretation be true to the other person's intention or sense of reality? Or is it only true to ours? Can we really know why another person is behaving a particular way without asking him or her? Can we believe them when our experience and assumptions tell us something different? When we interpret another's behavior without checking out our assumptions, we are only talking to ourselves and having a relationship with our own minds. Our actions and choices can seem inappropriate or strange to others because we haven't let them know what we are thinking. We haven't connected. This is a common occurrence in business even more than it is in our personal relationships. If we want a solid team and close relationships, we need to check out our assumptions. This can be difficult when we don't believe what another person tells us.

Is interpretation a given factor? Does everyone interpret? Probably. Yet, it is essential that a person who is searching for connection and a deeper sense of reality eliminates as many assumptions as he or she can. This greatly enhances the probability of success in communication and decision-making, allowing for Top Performance Leadership.

Need for Approval

Our need for approval comes from the "child" within us. What occurs when we allow another person to determine what is appropriate for us? Well, usually that decision erodes our confidence. It makes us feel small. We give up our knowledge of right and wrong and allow another to tell us what is best for us. We eventually blame him or her if things go wrong. Imagine yourself without a need for approval. Imagine yourself making mistakes and letting that be okay. Imagine not giving approval to others.

Imagine giving spontaneous acknowledgment and support rather than approval or disapproval.

The stories you tell yourself about why and how you think and act the way you do may protect you from this knowledge of your need for approval, although it was most likely necessary when you were a child. There is a cost for this protection. For some, it is emotional and spiritual prejudice. Denying responsibility gives our power to others and deepens and strengthens the shadow. Blaming parents or others for our feelings and experiences is an epidemic in our culture.

How will you ever live your purpose as a Top Performance Leader and maintain your passion if you keep giving away your power?

Beliefs

Once we become aware of our "shadow" and how we project that negativity or admiration on others, we can tackle our self-limiting beliefs about ourselves and take a look at our beliefs about leadership. Which of these beliefs seem to be yours?

Self-limiting Beliefs

1. I'm really not smart or capable enough to be the CEO of a company.
2. I want this promotion, but I don't think I have the wherewithal to be successful.

3. I'm too old to change my career and reach the top.

4. My dreams and obligations collide.

5. I can't change my personality.

6. I don't have the courage to risk the career move because it might hurt others.

7. I have spent my time in business trying to get ahead and fit into other's expectations. I can't be myself and get ahead.

8. There is not enough to go around.

9. I feel selfish and egotistical creating a vision for myself.

10. I don't need a vision. All is going well.

11. I don't have time to be inspired from within. I don't want to stop and take time out of my day.

12. I am afraid that if I have what I want, others may be hurt or I might quit my job or leave my family.

Beliefs about Leadership

1. Leaders have an innate ability that cannot be learned.

2. Leaders are lonely and alone.

3. Leaders need to be right to be respected.

4. Leaders lose influence when they make mistakes.

5. Leadership means being powerful and not showing vulnerability.

6. Leadership requires personal sacrifice.

7. Leaders cannot share their insecure thoughts because they will appear weak.

8. Leaders are smarter than others and get special breaks in life.

Beliefs Come from Somewhere

We enter this world needing to adapt to the culture of our families, and recent research shows this process is considered complete by the time we are three years old. So what does that have to do with Top Performance Leadership? When we are children, we adapt to our families' beliefs and values. In order to adapt, we take on our parents' beliefs to make sense of our feelings. The beliefs we form as children stay with us as long as they serve our purpose.

Think about your childhood for a moment. Do you remember promising yourself you would "never" or "always" say, do, or be just like your parents? I remember when my daughter was a teen and we were having an argument about her curfew. Before I could stop myself, I heard my mother's words coming out of my mouth. I felt shock. How could that occur? That happened more and more as my daughter matured into a young woman. I judged, interpreted, projected, and disapproved until I could make peace with my internal "mother." We all have internalized our parents. We can either reject or accept their teachings or we can personalize the same and become conscious of how they continue to affect us. When we reject their influence, they become an integral component of our shadow; when we simply accept, we stop growing. As we become aware of this phenomenon, we gain the ability to reclaim our free will.

As this awareness grows, we can see the original reasons that support our old beliefs while we create new ones. With this new understanding, you can grow to be a Top Performance Leader. Of course, challenges to new beliefs will arise. When they do, you can remember to hold as precious that new picture of yourself. As we choose beliefs based on fear, our dreams and desires move further away. As we remember who we are, we get closer to our dreams. No matter what your job, you can be a Top Performance Leader when you make decisions based on the present situation and challenge.

This can lead to a paradox. Have you ever heard of cognitive dissonance? This is a state of mind occurring when new information conflicts with what our mind previously held as true. The collision between the new information and the old creates mental agitation, perturbing the mind. It tends to last until the brain can adjust and accept the new reality.

You may have had this experience lately. It could be a need to both sleep in and work out during the same morning hours. It could be about eating healthy knowing you have diabetes, and wanting sugar at the same time. You might want to blame an associate for a mistake while knowing you are responsible and accountable. It could come from reading this book, wanting to reject the ideas presented while at the same time knowing they are valid. Allowing new information to replace old habitual thinking can create serious anxiety. Or it can be simple and easy.

Think of the cognitive dissonance that occurred when Copernicus proved that the earth orbited the sun. For centuries, people had believed the opposite, that the sun orbited the earth. So, Copernicus's new information caused all sorts of cultural and religious agitation. As a result, even though it was backed up by scientific data, it took a long time for the majority of people to accept the Copernican system.

When in cognitive dissonance, the brain feels over-loaded. Old beliefs can get shaken. Those beliefs that were taken as truth are now challenged and called into doubt. Even if the new information makes sense intellectually, when you try to apply it, it's difficult. It is not easy to shift to a new way of thinking. New levels of truths demand new solutions and behaviors.

What new truths have you discovered recently? How did you discover them? How will you act on them in your company? In your personal life?

It can be thorny confronting your judgments and beliefs. Many people cannot maintain a leadership position because they refuse to look at themselves. Responding to what is true with skillful action while it is going on in present time is the goal for Top Performance Leaders. Yet doing this will cause cognitive dissonance and discomfort. If you can allow your feelings and thoughts to coexist for a while, you will emerge stronger. By staying with the discomfort, it changes into new information that begins to make sense. What comes toward you will not be as daunting as you previously thought and you will be ready to let it come your way. These steps are vital precursors to your goal of being a Top Performance Leader.

We are aware that other authors have explored elements of the idea or belief of creating action based on reality, not the past. Ken Wilbur, Robert Ornstein, Marilyn Ferguson, and Peter Fenner each have looked at the role of awareness in effective living, and reading their works will give you other perspectives on this topic.

CHAPTER 2

RESPONSIBILITY AND INTEGRITY

We directly experience another person's responsibility and integrity when we are around him or her. Think about the times you were in the presence of an authentic leader.

Many years ago, I was consulting at a large multi-national bank and was privileged to meet with a trusted advisor and confidante of the CEO. After we were introduced and some pleasantries were exchanged, he rolled up his sleeves, looked me directly in the eye, and asked me what I thought it would take to heal the split between two competing factions of the organization. He knew I was there to be considered as a consultant for leadership development.

I remember being fearful of saying something politically incorrect and capitulated to being polite rather than honest. He interrupted me. He spoke of how he saw the situation as a father with two children, the bank being the father and the two divisions being the two children. I was surprised at the analogy. I was moved at how he was willing to share his personal opinions with me. I decided at that moment to be more forthcoming and honest with him. I talked about what it is like when children are the product of a divorce and a second marriage. I knew the two divisions were the results of mergers and acquisitions and that each harbored feelings of being the step-child.

Although I feel comfortable sharing personal opinions during coaching sessions and leadership trainings, I was hesitant to be so forthcoming in a first meeting with a client before we signed a contract. We began speaking of the obstacles to mergers based on the beliefs and values of the two organizations and why the larger organization needed to acquire rather than merge with the smaller one. He shared how he differed with the CEO on many values of the organization and how that would most likely determine his future. In fact, within that year, he asked to be transferred to England where he could add value to his work and organization without putting his career in jeopardy.

Being a Top Performance Leader in the twenty-first century is singularly different than ever before. Although all the old requirements still need to be fulfilled, many new requirements have emerged. There is a transformative quality that goes beyond today's mainstream perspective. The simplest way to describe this quality is through the concept of energy flow. Top Performer Leaders commit, focus, and give their full attention to what they are doing and who they are with. The old standard command-and-control mode is not viable, as it doesn't allow for conversation or dialogue; it is a one-way street that ends up at the end of the road.

Standing in integrity is an exhilarating experience; every option is equally doable and possible. Personal responsibility is the road to integrity. The elimination of "automatic pilot" behaviors and familiar patterns gives us the power to generate innumerable opportunities. The past is only one stream of information we act on when we are standing in integrity. Making the choice to be personally responsible alters the way the past affects us, and we are able to respond to what arises from the unique circumstances we are part of at that moment.

When our actions come from what naturally arises from the situation we are in, we experience congruence; our inside and outside match each other. Virginia Satir, a pioneer in family therapy, defines congruence as a balance between our self, the other, and the context of the situation. Congruence is having one face, a state of integrity occurring when we are aware of what we are putting into the world. Do our feelings and thoughts move to right action? Are these actions natural and sensible?

Having integrity entails staying aware of your internal state and making choices that naturally support your future. Most people separate their inner experience from the outer world. Our society thinks a lack of integrity is the same as conscious lying. In the context of Top Performance Leadership, integrity means being aware of your entire self, including your shadow (discussed in Chapter One). This means accepting the part of you that judges, projects, and is petty and nasty. Your reward is congruence, integrity, extremely positive results, and a good night's sleep.

Integrity	Lack of Integrity
• Vulnerability	• Denial
• Clarity	• Illusion
• Transparency (one face)	• Noncommittal (many-faced)
• Owning your shadow	• Projection
• Proactive	• Reactive
• Response-able	• Control
• Spontaneity	• Default
• Experience	• Interpretation

Some of the difficulty we have with integrity and personal responsibility is due to how our brains work. We filter what we see, hear, feel, and think through our past experiences and combine this with whatever is going on in the present. As a result, the present moment is affected by the past. Self-awareness and emotional intelligence disengages this repetitive cycle and allows you to use your present thoughts and feelings as data to make important decisions in a conscious manner, rather than through past experience.

A conscious, thoughtful response is an important aspect of freedom and Top Performance Leadership. An autopilot response only leads to a repetition of what came before.

Integrity and Responsibility in Business

Having integrity all the time is being responsible. Lack of personal responsibility and integrity in business is caused by pretending something did not happen. People often use denial as a way to avoid accountability. Those who are out of integrity say, "I don't know" when they don't want to say what they think. They are noncommittal. They take all sides. They are like a sail in a windy sea without a rudder.

Integrity and responsibility are precursors to Top Performance, allowing us to risk new behaviors that create new lives and organizations. Choosing these behaviors creates unlimited options and possibilities. We all have this opportunity.

Tools of personal responsibility
- Assume positive intent on the part of others
- Be in the present moment rather than in the past or the future
- Be willing to do what it takes to achieve excellent results
- Respond with one face
- Speak your truth
- Maintain congruence between words and actions

Examining personal responsibility

Please do this exercise:

- Identify a circumstance or relationship in your life that is not working. This can be personal or professional. It can range from an issue you have with a friend or colleague to a crisis in a team or in your company.
- Take a few minutes to get completely into the experience.
- Close your eyes. Notice your thoughts about this situation.
- Have you had these thoughts about other situations in the past? Are these thoughts familiar? Do you remember having them as a child?

Your thoughts that appear are not only from the present situation. They are compounded by all the similar-feeling situations in your life. We are not going to resolve those now. However:

- Can you see how this way of thinking will keep you stuck?
- Based on what you have read in previous chapters, and what arises now when you focus on this experience, what shift can you make in your thinking to give you clarity?

(Hint: Response Ability.)

Please take a moment to write down your responses.

_____

_____

_____

_____

Now, look again at the same situation. With this shift in your thinking, you will begin to do things differently. Can you think of a few situations that will be affected by this change?

Give your answer a chance. Make it work. See what happens.

When you are personally responsible, as in the above exercise, you will encounter less resistance from your peers, the people you manage, and those who manage you. Remember, resistance is a natural stage with any change. However, as you practice these skills and they become more like skin than clothing, you will notice the ease with which you are able to navigate resistance. This will help you grow in your career.

Achieving personal responsibility

Is there an easy way to achieve personal responsibility? The answer is yes and no. As discussed earlier in this chapter, a key factor for success is "cognitive dissonance," the ability to hold two opposing perspectives simultaneously. Your opposing thoughts and feelings will constantly vie for your attention as you make this shift into personal responsibility. They may be in direct opposition to your short-term goals or what you need to accomplish at any moment. If you find yourself in this paradox, you can learn to take the right action by letting go of personal preference. This is true emotional literacy and another skill of the Top Performance Leader.

When you become personally responsible, you are aware of your personal reactions to conflict, discomfort, frustration, confusion, embarrassment, anger, and more. For example, you may receive feedback and want to defend your position, explain yourself, argue, and prove you are right, sometimes all at once. What can you do to support yourself in these situations? Here are four key steps to follow that will help you remember your commitments to yourself: STOP, LOOK, LISTEN, and ACT.

1. STOP what you are doing. This is the most important step, because if you don't do this, it's over, you're on automatic pilot. As a leader, you don't want that. You want to be intentionally self-aware. Remember, you are always modeling the behavior you want to have from others.

2. LOOK at what is happening. What are you feeling? You may be angry, sad, frustrated, etc. Ask yourself why. This is where it can get sticky. If you are willing to tell yourself the truth, you will see the answer is about you, not someone else (even though you will

likely be able to produce evidence that it is about someone else). It is about you. So now that you've stopped yourself from behaving in a way you don't want to, you've also looked for and discovered the feelings that have surfaced. When you know your feelings, you can access the information that will help you make a positive decision.

3. LISTEN for the answer to what you want to accomplish right now. The information to let you know what you need will come to you . It is always aligned with your commitments and your values. The little voice that wants to get even, be on top, or be the powerful one is *not* the voice of your higher values.

4. Finally, ACT. Do the right thing. Take the high road and choose the correct behavior for the situation. You know what that is!

I'm not suggesting that you'll be able to do this perfectly every time, particularly in the beginning. But like everything else, the more practice the easier it gets, and consider the payoff.

CHAPTER 3

VISION

A Vision Is the Picture of Your Purpose Brought to Life

An original creation, whether it's a painting, a book, a family, or an organizational culture, arises from our imagination, starting with an idea or inspiration. When we imagine an idea or a vision and then see it take form, we are able to make the invisible become visible. It is the closest we come to being alchemists or magicians. Knowing that you can move an idea from its inception through the necessary steps to realization is essential for any success or accomplishment. You need to experience the truth of your vision for it to take shape in the world, and you must remain committed throughout the life of that vision. This is what Top Performance is about. These elements of imagination, belief, and commitment are essential to turn ideas and imagination into day-to-day success.

Remember when you were a kid and knew what captured your passion? Some of you enjoyed the idea of rescuing people from difficult situations. Others loved to win at board games and still others savored competing in sports. Many could sit with a science or math problem and have a conversation about diameters and radii. There were some who could just sink into an easy chair for an entire afternoon daydreaming and thinking. We were in tune with Einstein when he said, "Imagination is more important than knowledge." We intuitively knew that our imagination could lead us to great discoveries and unending accomplishment. This imagination also made each one of us an original.

Each of us has a unique capability. We each have our own set of dreams, beliefs, desires, and abilities. When these come together, we get extraordinary results. Top Performance Leaders are able to transform their personal and organizational vision into reality through effective action, while making space for others to do the same.

As you increase your intention and commitment as a leader, your clarity and focus also heighten.

You will naturally embody your vision when you demonstrate the value of your point of view through who you are as well as what you do. A Top Performance Leader is aware that understanding and knowledge without clear vision are neither efficient nor sustainable. They develop gripping, undeniable strategies for transforming business performance, and can generate results that appear extraordinary, no matter what the business environment.

To become a Top Performance Leader you hold a clear and powerful vision of your desired outcomes to guide your day-to-day decision making. Use your vision as the compass. Identify and take the correct action every time. If you examine your purpose and vision in the context of the larger organization's purpose and vision, you will learn how to create a shared vision.

A Case Study

One of my young sales people found an opportunity for our company to respond to a request for proposal (RFP) that really spoke to our hearts. We were a custom, creative shop that designed and delivered strategic learning solutions to Fortune 500 companies. We decided to compete for the project. Little did we know it would change the soul of our company. Although we had many over-$500,000 projects and, in fact, had companies that over the years paid us that amount many times over, we had never negotiated for more than that amount at one time.

We spoke with the COO of this company. Through a discovery process with him and a few other members of their organization, we helped them clarify their needs and qualification of the people for their project. They wanted to design a new corporate culture, including all of the programs and materials that go along with that. We were still a small company and I, as CEO, didn't know if we had the capability or capacity to take on a project of that size.

After meeting with my team, we decided to submit a proposal for the project. We made it to the finals. We were competing with well-known training organizations that were comfortable managing multimillion-dollar projects. We wanted to demonstrate our capability in the presentation rather than talk about it. This was the beginning of our Top Performance Leadership. We won the contract and thus began a two-year journey that taught me how to be an authentic, effective Top Performance Leader. The *pièce de résistance* came when I was meeting with the CEO at his organization, discussing final financial details.

Previous to being the CEO and president at Educational Discoveries, I was a psychotherapist, a workshop leader, and an academic. I was thrust into this leadership role at my company and was following the unspoken rules I thought were appropriate. So, when the CEO of the fitness company asked me how much gross profit we were making on this project, I panicked. Having heard others talk about not telling a client how much money we were making, I felt uncomfortable discussing this openly and told him so. He looked right at me and told me how important it was to his company that we were making enough money to allow us to perform at a top level of effectiveness. I had assumed he wanted to lower the amount of profit we were making. I was embarrassed. Where did my thought come from? What had made me respond based upon what others had said rather than what was true? How could I assume I knew what my client was thinking and then act on my assumptions without checking with him?

I did not have a personal vision until that time. I only had a vision of "what made sense" for my company with short and long-term goals. After that incident, I created my personal vision and aligned it with a company vision, and it was big enough to support me and Educational Discoveries, eventually becoming successful enough to be bought by Provant, a publicly held company. My personal vision was *ending child abuse by making the workplace healthy*. Our company vision was *bringing spirit back into the workplace*.

Finding Your Vision

Many people think that they do not have a personal vision or that their vision is not in step with that of their organization. Most of the time, this is not really the case. In T*he Empowered Manager*, Peter Block offers an effective approach for people who say they don't have a personal vision for themselves. He urges us not to believe them. Everybody is operating on a vision, whether they are aware of it or not. The following exercise will give you the opportunity to make your vision tangible.

First, do you have already have personal and/or a professional vision?

If so, please answer the questions below.

- What is it?

- Does it still work for you?
- Please describe it in the space provided below.

_____

_____

_____

_____

If not, let's create one now! You can change it any time you want, and you don't have to keep it. It is not written in stone or permanent ink. Your vision could be about a career, a financial windfall, a relationship, a change of course in your life. It doesn't matter if it is real or not. It does matters that you take a risk and do the exercise.

Let's do it.

Are you ready? Uncross your legs. Put your hands on your lap. Take a deep breath. Now take another one. Close your eyes and let your mind wander for a minute or so.

- Imagine having your deepest desire come true right now.
- Watch it take shape in your imagination.
- How do you feel? Picture yourself living this day to day.
- What will your life be like? What stops you from having this?
- Commit to it.
- Think about how it can guide you through difficult times and future obstacles.

- Consider the challenges and resistance that may arise.
- Remember, a vision is a picture of a purpose brought to life in present time. What is your vision? Can it be stated in a sentence? Remember, you can revisit the vision as many times as you wish, until you feel comfortable, until it fits.
- Please write down the vision you receive from this excercise.

_____

_____

_____

_____

For a few people, this exercise provides immediate access to a vision. People who are able to easily answer the questions leading to a clear vision are usually doing what Steven Covey emphasized when he said, "Begin with the end in mind!" They naturally lead their lives in this way. It is not right or wrong. It is just natural for them at this time of their development as leaders.

For many people, however, this exercise can be disappointing. It may be difficult to construct clear and coherent answers to the questions. These people may be moving indirectly toward a vision. No matter. It is difficult to create a vision under pressure, for example. Also, there are many self-limiting beliefs we have that stop us from moving out of our patterns. Top Performance cannot occur when we continue to be automatic in our behaviors—we need to be inspired. What inspires you? How do you behave when you are inspired?

Borrow a vision

If you don't have a vision yet, it is not a problem. Sometimes it helps to borrow a vision first.

Here are a few to choose from. You can "lease" one until you are ready to create your own.

1. A prosperous year for my company and family
2. A process-based company where employees come first
3. A balanced work and home life
4. A fit, healthy body

Let your vision be your guide

Imagine that you are walking along a road in the country-side. You come to a fork in the road. There are two paths to choose from. At first glance, both paths look similar. You look to the left and see beautiful trees and flowers as well as homes and stores. You look to the right and see beautiful trees and flowers and homes and stores as well. You look back to the left and now you notice many familiar signs you've seen before. Because it is familiar, it pulls you to it. You know how to navigate that road.

Now you look to the right and although it still looks

appealing, the signs are written in another language, one not familiar to you. In fact, as you continue to look, you have a feeling of apprehension. You realize if you follow this road to the right, you're on a new adventure. And if you go left, you're more likely to know your way.

You take the familiar road. You know where to go, where to turn, how to find the way. It is safe. The other road, where the signs are in another language, presents a challenge. You don't know where it will lead. You continue along that path and end up where you have been many times in your life. You go back to the fork.

What choice will you make now? If you go back to the road that is familiar, you know what to expect and how to behave. It will bring you to the same place you just found yourself, to the same choices you have made time and time again. If you choose the unfamiliar path, you will need to stay awake and aware. You will need to learn how to read the signs and what direction to take.

You have not traveled this path before. There will be times when you will wish you had taken the familiar path, when you will feel uncomfortable at your not knowing. That is when your personal vision and your team will guide you. Your vision serves as an inspiration and a reminder that you made a choice to go on a new journey. You will find your way. You have up to now.

CHAPTER 4

LISTENING AND COMMUNICATING

HOW TO SAY AND HEAR EVERYTHING

What is Communication?

Communication is the exchange of information. Effective communication is a two-way, genuine connection between people. It creates engagement and alignment and results in a positive working relationship, with synergy and success as the natural outcomes.

Most communication theorists agree that words make up less than 10 percent of communication. Body language, tone, and facial expressions are considered more important than any literal understanding of words. Everything you say and do communicates a complex message. A simple shake of the head or a raising of an eyebrow can send each person in the room into his or her private world of meaning.

There is also a well-developed, complex language communicated beneath the words, in any interaction, understandable through "emotional literacy." This language is emotional, energetic, powerful, and useful. The more aware you are of this type of communication, the clearer your message is received and the clearer is the message you communicate. You experience this whenever you meet a new person or go to someone's home or look in someone's eyes. We call this our intuition; we say we are psychic or use some other name. In fact, it may be all of those. It is occurring all the time.

Effective communication is essential for delivering superior results. It helps keep everyone informed and feel a part of things. In fact, when a leader is consistent and communicates clearly, listeners don't ever have to think about what is being said. They understand the meaning behind the words, so the message strikes home.

When communication is out of balance, with a lack of congruence or integrity, and people are not saying all there is to say, much goes "undercover." This usually creates divisiveness and unproductive chaos. It eventually becomes part of the shadow of the organization. When this happens, the very foundations of the relationships in the company are at stake (although it could take years to go from an initial incongruous communication to the final dilemma).

Finances, sales, or production, can be affected long after the communication problems occurred. Does that seem difficult to accept and believe? Just take a look at many of the mammoth organizations in America and the condition they are in. Now, remember the time when their troubles began to be reported. Look at their stock prices and compare them to companies that are more nimble and have open communication.

Take a moment to think about what happens in an organization when messages that need to be delivered are not made clear to the person concerned.

- Does this happen in your organization?
- Does this happen to you? Do you have unspoken concerns?
- What do you need to say?
- Who do you need to say it to?
- Why is it important?

What is your company saying to all who encounter it? What is the unspoken message when someone calls or walks into the organization? Nothing really goes unnoticed by co-workers or customers, though there may be agreements to not notice things.

As a Top Performance Leader, you need to pay attention to what is going on in your area of operation and seek input. As you allow communication to unfold in the form of inputs, you will notice that the intensity of these concerns will lessen and work will become easier, more collegial and aligned. There could be changes in your life due to the unfolding of authentic communication between you and the people that surround you in your work and home. You might decide that the role you play at your organization needs to change, or you might decide to resign. You may realize you simply need to say what was on your mind and didn't know how to do this in an effective manner. Before you take any action, check your communication with the people concerned using the tools this chapter provides.

Content and Context

Many people think that the content of a communication is more important than the context in which it is presented, even when they have had experiences over and over that show that to be untrue.

Context is the intellectual, emotional, and physical environment that surrounds the communication and provides meaning to the listener. Context creates an orientation, so people know why they are receiving the information, its value to them personally, and what the information has to do with the "big picture." Do you know what it is like to receive information from a negative place? How about from a positive standpoint? How about neutral?

The tone and intent of your message is experienced by people even if you are unaware of what you are feeling or thinking at that moment. If, for example, the tone of a communication is cold or hostile, the listener will resist receiving it. In fact, the listeners can create a cloud around themselves that seems impenetrable. They will hear something other than what you intend to communicate. I am certain you have had that experience at some point—I have. When I talk with people who are skeptical, I begin to doubt what I am saying . . . unless I stay aware of myself in their presence. If I am not self-aware at that time, I may believe the other person is "making" me feel skeptical. When I talk with someone who is interested in my perspective, and I in theirs, we are having a meaningful conversation on our way to establishing a meaningful relationship. I want to talk with them more. I enjoy those discussions. I may remember what they said when I am in situations that call their thoughts to my mind.

Think about being with someone you trust and who trusts you. Now, imagine a conversation with him in which he brings up something negative or critical about you. He says it in a joking manner. Most of the time, you will laugh, knowing he is sharing his thoughts from a caring space and he is not judging you. But this same conversation with the same content would be entirely different with a person you do not trust. Why? What makes the difference for you? Do you feel vulnerable? Do you feel embarrassed? Here are some tools that may make it easier to connect to these conversations.

Tools for Communication
Buy-in
What does it mean to "buy-in" to something?

Buy-in is ownership. You know exactly how you feel when you believe in an idea or a company or anything.

You own it. You've seen it and you believe in it so strongly that it's yours. So buy-in is literally the process by which a person takes or gets ownership of an idea or a concept.

What Is Buy-in?

Buy-in is the process by which people take ownership. It begins with having passion and intention. The next step is finding the words, questions, or interactions that cause others to become interested in supporting a new idea or action. The outcome of buy-in is that the listener has taken ownership of the idea or action for his personal reasons as well as yours, and can answer the question, "What does it mean to me personally?"

When Do You Use It?

• Any time you need other people's active support for a new idea, change, or behavior

• When you want to motivate an individual or a team

• When you need participation from others in an idea or action

Why Do You Use It?

People participate with more enthusiasm and creativity when they "buy-in" and feel included and involved, especially when the process allows them to express their concerns or skepticism. It makes the leader's job easier because it lets you know where your people stand. They feel included and tend to become your allies. Once people can align their personal values with something at their work, they become involved and interested.

How Do You Use It?

Use personal experiences, stories, questions, and authentic listening that addresses the challenges and dreams you and your listeners have in common. If there is likely to be some resistance or concern with the new idea, address both the benefits and the pitfalls of the new challenge from a neutral point of view. If you are in a situation where you have to "present" something with little or no interactive discussion, make sure you are clear in what you say and that your message appeals to both the heart and mind of your listeners. Whenever possible, conduct an interactive discussion where your listeners are actively involved and doing most of the talking. Your main job is to ask stimulating and provocative questions, and listen carefully to what your listener says.

What gets you to buy-in? It happens when something makes sense to you. If you want another to take ownership for something new, it's important to talk with them about it in a way that makes sense and appeals to their sense of worth. Do it without trying to convince them. Think about how you perceive someone when it's clear they are a little too persuasive and want to convince you. Aren't you a little more resistant right off the bat? A little suspicious?

You have to ask yourself, "What is the real value of this project, idea, product, to me?" before you can get someone else to buy-in. Put yourself in someone else's shoes. It's not just about your agenda; you also have to include their agenda, their concerns, and what is meaningful to them.

Although this may appear to be difficult at first, using these tools makes it easier.

The next tool is common ground.

Common ground

We all have a sense of common ground. It's what you share with someone else, something you can build on. You can also use common ground to recognize what is *not* common between yourself and others, and work to establish this connection.

Common ground can be created or established in a lot of different ways, just like buy-in. When you use buy-in questions to get people to share their experiences, it can create an experience common to everyone.

What is Common Ground?

Common ground is the content or experiences shared by associates that give them a sense of belonging to a team. Establishing common ground with others creates a connection, allowing people to unite in a common goal.

When Do You Use It?

• Any time you want to introduce a new idea or change.

• Any time you want to create buy-in.

• Whenever there is a sense of confusion or lack of focus in your team.

• Whenever people seem to be working at cross-purposes.

Why Do You Use It?

When you are introducing something new, listeners need to be able to relate *to it in a personal way. When you create common ground, your listener will feel like they're "on the same page" with you. It will be easier for them to join in and accept your ideas.*

How Do You Use It?

Ask questions or share experiences that allow you and your listener to discover common ground. Maybe you've held the same job as the person or people you're talking to, or you like the same sports team. Give examples that people can relate to from their experience. Share experiences or stories that allow people to connect to you personally, and to the topic you are introducing. Martin Luther King did this in his "I Have a Dream" speech. He talked about his dream in terms we can all identify with.

The ideal result of creating common ground is that your audience says to themselves, "I can relate to that," or "Wow, this person really understands my situation and can appreciate it." And you do!

Common ground creates relevance for people. When it comes right down to it, people are much more alike than different. So common ground has many benefits. Fundamentally, it means you meet people where they are. Before I move on to the next tool, I want to connect and relate the first two tools so far—buy-in and common ground.

What is the relationship between buy-in and common ground?

Essentially, establishing common ground with a person or group is one method of getting buy-in. It might not be everything that you need, but it can help you get buy-in.

Think about it—if the other person doesn't feel like they're sharing anything in common with you in that moment, how will you get buy-in for anything?

So, finding the common ground is one way to get buy-in.

Asking questions

Asking questions is a process that allows you to gather real information from people and find out more of the truth about something. It also lets you see how people think and allows them to experience how you think. As a Top Performance Leader, this is a necessity.

When you ask questions, give space and permit the listener to make their own connections to what is required of them, thus creating feelings of ownership and motivation in them.

Why is this valuable? People tend to be more involved and participative when they discover their own answers.

What Is Asking Questions?

Asking questions is a process that allows you to gather real information from people, rather than assuming that you already know what you need to know. This process allows you and your listener to "discover" both the obvious and non-obvious truths about a situation.

When Do You Use It?

- *When you want to create more involvement and participation.*
- *When you need to discover what's motivating other people's thinking or behavior.*
- *When you want people to discover an important learning for themselves, rather than being told.*

Why Do You Use It?

Asking questions helps make information more relevant, personal, and memorable to the listener, because they discover answers for themselves rather than having solutions provided. Questions help create ownership and motivation to act. Your listener is more engaged and attentive. Questions help create a partnership between you and the listener.

How Do You Use It?

- *Think about what's important to you and to your listener and ask questions about the key issues you share.*
- *Listen with an open heart and mind to how the other person responds.*
- *Continue asking questions and be part of an interactive dialogue that deals authentically with the situation.*

If you don't ask questions and gather real information about what's going on, you are operating on assumptions and interpretations.

When you make assumptions, there's a very good chance you're assuming wrongly. We tend to project our own motivations and scenarios onto someone else when we make assumptions. When in doubt, check it out—by asking questions. A Top Performance Leader needs to check all of his/her assumptions before acting.

The next tool is Listening.

Listening

What Is Listening?

Listening is akin to receiving. It means remaining open and neutral to what is communicated, and not changing what you hear in your own mind as you receive it. Listening includes hearing words as well as hearing what's underneath the words. This is the philosopher's stone of the all the tools listed here.

When Do You Use It?

• *When you want to create a relationship*
• *When you want or need to get information*
• *Whenever anyone is communicating something to you*

Why Do You Use It?

Listening creates and strengthens connections among team members, managers, peers, and customers. By listening, you receive new information all the time—ideas, how people experience you, expectations of you, questions. An authentic response to asking a question is listening to the answer. These new experiences that come from listening to another and allowing their information in create synergy in a natural manner.

How Do You Use It?

Use both your heart and mind to listen. That means be open and neutral to the information given to you. This is when your ego may feel bruised. Is that okay? Choose how to respond to a communication only after you've really listened.

When we actually listen to someone, we can recognize what's going on in his life in many ways, including subtleties and that which is apparent. We can also better understand our own needs and concerns, help to build relationships, and know how to give what is needed.

Have you ever been asked a question and then not been listened to? What impact has that had on you? What is the difference when you are asked a question and *are* listened to?

So, here's the message—do *not* ask questions unless you're going to listen. Do you want your team members to trust you, and have an experience that you are genuine? Then really follow that rule. Do *not* ask questions unless you are going to listen.

Do you think you will be viewed as genuine if you don't listen to how your team responds to your questions? Consider what happens when you do listen.

Here are some keys to effective listening:

- Listen with a neutral, open heart and mind. This allows you to focus on what others mean. This can be difficult, as most of the time we don't have a totally open mindset.

- Hear the genuine concerns of the person.
- Pay attention to the content of what the person is saying, but also pay attention to *how* they say it, if you want to discover their true feelings about the subject.
- Don't interrupt. Wait until you've heard the entire message before you decide how to respond.
- Reserve judgment. Respond with what arises after you have heard the other person.

Discovery

By asking questions, we allow the listener to "discover" solutions or answers rather than providing them with our own solutions. It helps them to take responsibility for taking action. When they discover solutions themselves it supports commitment.

For example, when you're conducting a performance review with an employee, it's helpful to get him to discover what you notice about his performance without just "telling" him. You can do this by asking him questions about his experience or about what he sees. In general, when a person doesn't feel judged or criticized, he is better able to discover what needs to occur to improve his performance.

What is Discovery?

Discovery is the process that allows the listener to uncover solutions rather than having solutions provided to him. It supports him to take responsibility for his own success. When we discover solutions ourselves, we become more committed to action.

When Do You Use It?

When you want people to realize an important lesson for themselves rather than being told.

Why Do You Use It?

To help the listener take ownership for what he is being asked to do. When he discovers his own solutions, he is more engaged, attentive, and involved in the process.

How Do You Use It?

Think about what's important to you and to your listener and ask questions accordingly. Then wait for the listener to answer. This facilitates his finding a solution himself and consequently taking responsibility for what he will do.

Level of accountability

This refers to the degree of significance, challenge, or risk that is involved for a person to participate in what you are asking him to do, and what results he will be personally responsible for producing.

JUDITH ORLOFF, MEd

For example, companies sometimes go through periods of rapid change and chaos. As a Top Performance Leader in that situation, there will be many different aspects on which you'll need to get your employees' buy-in. Some of them will be relatively easy for your employees to accept, while others may be quite difficult. Asking employees who have been part of a patriarchal organization to become personally accountable, for example, is a change that is difficult.

What Is Level of Accountability?

Level of Accountability refers to the degree of significance, challenge, or risk that is involved for a person to participate in what you are asking him to do. It also includes the results that he will be personally responsible for producing.

When Do You Use It?

You need to be aware of the Level of Accountability at all times, both with regard to what you are asking the other person to do, and what factors may affect his ability to agree. Awareness of this allows you to continuously adjust your communication to the reality of your listener's experience and ability so that he doesn't become bored, frustrated, judgmental, or overwhelmed.

Why Do You Use It?

You want to be able to communicate with people at the correct Level of Accountability so that they can understand your message. If you are unaware of this you may be talking over their heads or, conversely, talking about things they already know and don't need to hear repeated. If the

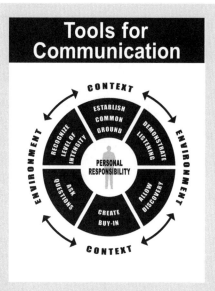

intensity of the discussion is too high, they may jump out of the boat, and if it is too low, they may mutiny.

How Do You Use It?

Again, put yourself in the shoes of the other person. Ask yourself, "What is it I want this person to be able to do?" Then position your communication accordingly. For example, when you talk to an employee about being late to work, the Level of Accountability is less than when you talk to him/her about a corrective action situation. When the Level of Accountability is very high, you'll want to take more care in setting the proper context for the communication by using the tools outlined in this chapter.

Once you understand the tools of communication, the following gap analysis for your organization may be useful. A gap analysis lets you know what is missing in the areas you are studying and how to fill it in with meaningful steps and information.

Communication Gap Analysis for Yourself and Your Organization

Consider the present condition at your organization (including attitude, knowledge, and management support) with regard to effective communication as described in this chapter. Now consider your desired result with regard to effective communication. Is there a gap? Most likely there is.

How will you bridge this gap. The best approach is to allow solutions to arise and unfold in the natural movement of ideas, while addressing at least three major elements:

1. Attitude

2. Knowledge

3. Management support

Understanding the difference between content (the what) and context (the how) along with effectively implementing the tools of communication is essential to becoming a Top Performance Leader.

CHAPTER 5

CONFLICT AND CHANGE

A FORCE OF NATURE

Conflict

In the book *Aikido, the Magic of Conflict*, Tom Crum says that conflict, in the form of earthquakes, hurricanes, and tornados, is a constant, natural force in nature. Conflict is also present throughout our lives, from wet diapers causing irritation, to learning multiplication tables, to learning new skills in a job or a relationship. Often our experience of conflict comes from our own simultaneous yet incompatible desires and drives.

Conflict is a source of creative energy. We experience it when we are searching for new solutions to problems and our innovative findings conflict with old ways of looking at a "stuck" situation. As we resolve that conflict we are richer in our knowledge and can find practical solutions that work for the organization.

It can also be a source of division, tension, backbiting, and sabotage. Much of the time, our response to conflict causes internal paralysis, lack of movement, and a narrow range of responses which seem limited to either/or, black or white. When our responses are in opposition to someone else's perspective or truth, we easily resort to arguments, judgments, and logjams that can result in distrust and loss of relationships. Many people respond to these situations with illness, feelings of disconnection, and a strong sense of isolation.

Why does this happen? What stops us from approaching these normal, natural life situations with ease and grace? We are certainly not limited to a narrow range of response and reactions and yet we behave much of the time as if we are powerless to make any change in how we respond. Why do we behave as if we are powerless to respond in a new way? Usually the source of this feeling of powerlessness to make new choices is our point of view of survival from early childhood. We will approach this through a business model. Consider the statement: either/or choices are dangerous to us personally and dangerous to our business as well.

And now, consider the following statements about conflict:

- When conflict escalates to a fight, the reason lies with the person who is doing the fighting, not the person with whom they are fighting.
- Becoming accountable for your resentments and imagined slights usually ends the internal conflict.
- No matter what the other party is doing or how it looks, we are responsible for our response. We can respond any way we wish.

- Discovering how we are the source of our uncomfortable feelings, instead of blaming them on the other person, brings great personal power and the freedom to act in new ways. For example, a need to be right hinders the creative exchange of ideas, while being open to someone else being right can create synergy and teamwork.

- This need to be right often produces what are perceived as insults and inflexibility on the part of the other person when in reality they stem from our own insecurities.

- Discriminating between internal conflicts and external relationships can end fights. Sabotage can disappear in a moment.

- Serious conflict saps energy, reduces efficiency, increases mistakes, and wastes time.

Do you agree with the above statements? If not, how would you change them? Looking at resolving conflict by realizing the above statements and acting on them will be beneficial and stress-reducing.

Ilya Prigogine, a Belgian physicist and Nobel Laureate chemist, is noted for his work on complex systems. I was curious about his work on creating order out of chaos, and was fortunate to meet with him when he spent some time in Boulder. Educational Discoveries' change model relating to individuals and organizations proved very similar to Dr. Prigogine's work in the areas of biology and physics. He believes that future results are not predictable from knowing the initial conditions of a situation. We agree with him and know from experience that break-through and transformation are possible at any moment. The potentiality of the moment resolves itself by the action we take.

This theory goes against the conventional knowledge that the past unavoidably conditions the future. Our perspective changes the idea of past history to the experience of the present moment. What we do in the present moment will condition the next moment, and then the next throughout all time. Operating from that perspective creates an antidote to powerlessness. When the positive aspect of conflict becomes a force of transformation, any moment seized with new behaviors and new thinking can produce extraordinary results.

> *"Leadership complements management: it doesn't replace it."*
> —John P. Kotter

Change

What kind of change have you experienced recently? It could be a new role in your company, a new job, a divorce, or relocation. How have you managed this change? Looking back, what were the events that made this change inevitable? If you knew then what you know now, what would you have done differently? If you had known that reactions and chaos were part of a natural process during this change, you may have been in a better position to manage it. There are many advantages to having a working model for change. A model acts as a roadmap and provides safety to the left brain.

Our model for change includes nine steps. In order to experience it, please choose a situation you are in at this time that you would like to see changed, and use this situation to take you through the nine steps. After you complete this exercise, you will see change has an easily recognizable pattern. You will be able to identify where you and your coworkers, direct reports, and managers are in this process. You will know that making changes are choices, no matter who or what initiates it. They can be deliberate self-aware actions living in the present moment or reactive responses living from proddings or the past.

A Model for Change
Step 1. The decision to change
Whether it is driven from a personal desire or an external necessity, you recognize the need to change. You decide to move forward, and leave the status quo.

You need to have a clear vision of what you want, the desire and will to make it happen, and a strong intention and the support to carry it through. (See Chapter 3 on how to formulate your vision.)

- What is the change you wish to make?
- What will accomplishing this change look like? How will it affect your personal life? Your professional life?
- Are your intentions for yourself and your company aligned to each other?

Step 2. Resistance

When you decide to change, you will likely encounter inner resistance. You may want to forget the change and go back to what is familiar. Resistance is equal parts order and chaos. Order represents the familiar—what was true before you made this decision. Chaos represents the new—the unknown. Whatever the degree of change desired, we usually match it with an equal degree of limiting beliefs that have stopped us making this change in the past. Change becomes a threat to our core belief system, the beliefs we have carried with us all our lives. Recognize that you will likely face some inner resistance when you decide to make this change.

Step 3. A choice point

When we are at a choice point, our agitation is strong; we either choose the past or choose to go forward into the unknown. When we do nothing, we choose the past.

Step 4. Illusion

If you choose not to move forward and instead choose the

past, you will enter a state of layered illusion. Choosing the past cannot work for you in the long term. If the past was workable there would be no need to change in the first place. Choosing the past repeatedly results in a self-deception, or illusion. You may deceive yourself into thinking the change was not necessary, or think you have already achieved it. This self-deceptive behavior eventually erodes your self-esteem. Being in a state of illusion can feel comfortable at first, yet it always involves faulty thinking. Believing that faulty thinking permeates many aspects of your life. It can become more global in its effects and over time can create the experience of crisis.

Step 5. Creating a crisis

Crisis does not occur suddenly. We can become used to living in a personal illusion. If you consistently choose illusion or the past, you become blinded to what you are doing and eventually create a crisis. Remember, what you did in the past does not work—that's why you made a decision to change in the first place. Prior to any crisis, there are many opportunities to move forward into the reality of the moment. The purpose of the crisis is to wake you up, so you can be responsible and make the changes you have committed to. You can recommit to making the change; be willing to take more risks and know you are not alone. There are many others feeling exactly what you are right at the same time.

Step 6. The chaos of creation

Rather than stay in the past, you can risk the unknown; take a new path and stay with your intention to change. This choice throws you into the chaos of creation rather than a crisis. You are in a state of paradox, maintaining two seemingly opposite experiences at once: chaos, because you are being pulled in opposite directions; creation, because now that you're in the unknown, you can see the pathway to choose new behaviors. This is where you learn to simultaneously acknowledge the past at the same time you are creating the future by staying with your decision to change, no matter how you feel inside.

Being in chaos is being open to new information while simultaneously feeling uncomfortable and unsure. You experience new information that was hidden by solidified patterns. In the chaos of creation, you choose a new reality by the focus and intention of your will to be in the present situation. You get another choice at this point: You can continue with your new choices or retreat again into your comfort zone of old patterns. You also have the experience of chaos of creation and can recognize it the next time you move toward crisis. You can then choose chaos rather than crisis.

Step 7. Support

Strong intention from you and support from others is critical for your change to manifest. It is easy to lose sight of your vision and fool yourself into going back to the old pattern. You need the support of people who know you and can help you stay on track. Allowing people to share what they observe about you helps you align with your decision to change. Also asking for help gives people the opportunity to give to you. You know how good it feels to give another support and to have them receive it.

Step 8. Responsibility

You have taken responsibility for your experiences. You are now aware that you are the source of your experience and you can receive and use new information. You see things from a new perspective. The old situations and circumstances have new meaning. You don't blame anyone, including yourself. In fact, you feel free.

Step 9. Breakthrough

Life doesn't feel, look, or seem familiar. Right now, it probably doesn't fit your image of how things are when you are close to achieving your goal, that is, the change you have been looking for. At this point, you need to remember your decision and intention, remembering what you have learned so far. So, although you may feel hesitant, if you stay on course, you can experience integrity and unimpaired ability. You are having the new experiences mentioned earlier. You are now true to your vision and intention. You will be ready for the next change when it presents itself.

Thriving in Paradox

A paradox is a situation that seems absurd or contradictory, but in fact is or may be true. Most of us are not able to process two or more opposing concepts without going a little crazy, especially when both of them seem valid and equal in value. And when it comes to leadership for the Top Performer, especially during the periods of conflict and change, the idea of paradox and the experience of its precessional effects become even more crucial. Although you might feel extreme emotions and antithetical ideas, you will be able to thrive throughout.

Paul Robertson, a senior consultant at the Cutter Consortium innovative practice, spent thirty-four years as founder and leader of the internationally acclaimed Medici Quartet. He says that being reflective in the moment while staying in the situation of paradox is a precursor to Top Performance Leadership. He says "you can learn to enjoy a leadership process that harnesses uncertainty to stimulate the vital creative energy your organization needs to be innovative and remain competitive."

In the previous chapter on conflict and change, we saw that crisis leads us directly to the "chaos of creation." Why do we need a crisis to give us license to make a change? Why can't we maintain high self-esteem while allowing others to be who they are even when we are very different from them? What is it about holding more than one concept in our minds, as in case of a paradox, that makes us falsely assume that something is wrong with the world?

Understanding how people move toward ownership of ideas and change may allow us to actually thrive in paradox. There is an ownership curve that occurs in organizations in periods of conflict and/or change that moves through the stages of awareness, understanding, buy-in, commitment, and finally, ownership. These stages parallel the steps in the model for change. The ownership curve was developed by Educational Discoveries along with a very large financial institution on the East Coast.

Where the model for change is an individual process, the ownership curve is operative for the organization as a whole.

Awareness

At this stage, we:

- encounter the signs of change and realize it is inevitable
- have a high level of awareness of the content and context of the process of change itself
- comprehend the nature and intent of the change as well as other people's roles in it
- are aware of the upcoming changes

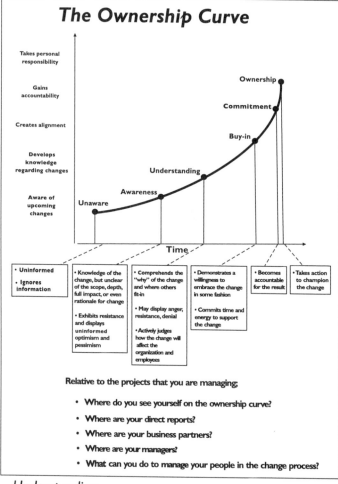

The Ownership Curve

Takes personal responsibility

Gains accountability

Creates alignment

Develops knowledge regarding changes

Aware of upcoming changes

Unaware — Awareness — Understanding — Buy-in — Commitment — Ownership

Time

| • Uninformed
• Ignores information | • Knowledge of the change, but unclear of the scope, depth, full impact, or even rationale for change

• Exhibits resistance and displays uninformed optimism and pessimism | • Comprehends the "why" of the change and where others fit-in

• May display anger, resistance, denial

• Actively judges how the change will affect the organization and employees | • Demonstrates a willingness to embrace the change in some fashion

• Commits time and energy to support the change | • Becomes accountable for the result | • Takes action to champion the change |

Relative to the projects that you are managing;

- **Where do you see yourself on the ownership curve?**
- **Where are your direct reports?**
- **Where are your business partners?**
- **Where are your managers?**
- **What can you do to manage your people in the change process?**

Understanding

At this stage, we:

- accept the nature and intent of the change
- understand many factors that are creating the change

- accept the display of anger, frustration and resistance
- develop knowledge and actively seek information to better understand the change

Participation

In the stage of participation, we:

- work toward the desired change by testing the new concepts and implications
- are influential and able to negotiate the desired result
- articulate our commitment to the change
- demonstrate a willingness to embrace the change
- create alignment personally and with others

Commitment

At this stage, we:

- articulate the change as an accepted norm
- articulate personal ownership of the change
- support others to be accountable

Ownership

In the ownership stage, we:

- identify new possibilities and approaches and act on them
- achieve measurable business results
- take personal responsibility for the change

Now you have experienced the model for change and understood the ownership curve, how to let go of conflict, and how to move through obstacles to results. It is time to move forward and make results happen in your organization.

CHAPTER 6

INTENTION, MOTIVATION, AND INFLUENCE

A Top Performance Leader can be located anywhere in your organization, from a CEO to a receptionist or maintenance worker. Many companies we have worked with create a "vertical slice" of employees across the organization that have similar qualities and can create a productive, exciting, high-performance environment for their peers. These people work as a team of equals. Roles and status in the organization are toned down so that each team member is equal in obligation, responsibility, and accountability. This does not mean they are equal in power or decision making or that they get the same pay. They may be called "change agents," "process leaders," "transformation conduits," or any name the particular organization is using.

Rosabeth Moss Kantar, professor of business administration at Harvard Business School, and author of *Confidence: How Winning Streaks & Losing Streaks Begin & End*, describes the culture and dynamics of top performance organizations. One of her key points is that the leaders in these organizations successfully use influence and motivation as means to ensure results.

Traditionally, these were learned skills and techniques or inherent characteristics of charismatic leaders. When you create an environment of top performance, effectiveness and motivation are the natural results. Authentic, congruent intention is what creates the difference between those who achieve Top Performance Leadership and those who have it simply as a preference in their minds. Our true intentions are always caught by others, even though our words and actions may be saying something else. Remember, words comprise only 10 percent of any communication. We can tell how clear our intentions have been by looking at our results.

Intention is the power and the steering. Without it, motivation to achieve cannot occur. Intention is always present, aligned with your desire. It is important to know which desire is steering your intention. Until you clarify your vision and purpose in your company, you are likely to go off course easily, especially into areas of personal comfort.

For example, I enjoy learning about my computer; it becomes a pastime for me. It is very comfortable for me to explore software and other gadgets. Yet I have deadlines and projects to complete. I need to be careful not to let my desire for recreation take precedence when I turn on my computer to work. So, I deliberately create my intention and then am motivated to act. Intention is there for motivation to attach itself to. You intend and then are motivated to act.

Vision Is the Vehicle

Intention Is the Steering

Motivation Is the Fuel

Influence Is the Passenger

Choice Is the Driver

Success Is the Destination

As a Top Performance Leader, you set the tone for everyone in your sphere of influence.

Your actions demonstrate the accepted behavior for those people. This is where the "law of idiosyncratic credits" takes hold: the higher up you are in the organization, whether by role attainment or by wielding influence, the more "credits" you acquire. This "law" is an important one. I have always enjoyed observing it in effect.

For example, imagine that the president appeared at a state meeting wearing sweats. How would this affect the standards of business dress in our country? Or, imagine what might have happened in your company if the CEO

Hollander, (1986), advanced the "idiosyncratic credit" model of leadership. According to this model, leaders earn such credits from follower's perceptions of their leader's competence and loyalty. A leader can then utilize such credits or trust to ensure commitment to innovative goals.

was seen having a high-protein drink after riding his bicycle to work each morning. Do you think there would be changes in the preferred mode of transportation? To make it more relevant, think about how you would be influenced if a leader in your company authentically shared his perspective when asked a question rather than giving a company line. Would you be motivated to do the same?

So, how does this really work? Many leaders harbor the intention to create group synergy for their team or peers. They plan their work well. They think about each person on a team and what needs to be done to have them work together well. They read up on others who have accomplished this. They write presentations using inspirational quotes, plan group activities to go along with the presentations, and expect success. Sounds great, doesn't it? It should be a breeze. So, why doesn't it happen? What goes wrong?

Let's look at what intention, motivation, and influence mean and how they work together.

- Intention is the state of having a purpose in mind.
- Motivation is a reason or incentive to do something.
- Influence is the power to affect something.

Bank of America introduced a new nationwide campaign to effectively attract new clients, respond to clients' needs, and more efficiently deliver a full array of products and services all at a profit to the bank. This type of process-centered culture, where leadership was based on a model of influence, was in contrast to how work historically had been performed with traditionally placed leaders. It required trustworthy people to collaborate with each other, take ownership of the new vision, be personally responsible, and continuously improve the process. For the process leaders, this meant learning new tools, skills, and ways of thinking and acting to create this type of top performance environment to successfully deliver the desired business results. On top of this, it is important to know that Bank of America is consistently in a chaotic environment created by uncompromising mergers and acquisitions and their drive for excellence.

The leadership model at the bank was previously based on command and control. It worked well for a long time. However, it was outdated and therefore ineffective in a process environment. For the strategy to be successful there needed to be a clear vision, strong clear intention, an inspirational motivation, a strong influence, shared goals and clearly defined benchmarks for success. The team that designed and developed this strategy (and the programs to implement it) needed to coordinate and become aware of their fears, challenges, and strengths. They did. This allowed them to react positively to feedback. They were able to build a culture of trust, equality, and personal responsibility.

Without self-awareness and a strong desire to be emotionally intelligent, a change of this nature would be fraught with undue complications. With motivation and clear purpose, the influence of a top performing leader is immense. He or she creates a synergy of intention, motivation, and influence, and the results are remarkable.

A Process for Influencing and Negotiating

1. Know and be aware of your own interests, needs, and positions.
2. Discover others' interests, needs, and positions by using enlightened dialogue:
   - Ask open questions.
   - Listen to the responses as well as what is implied by the words.
   - Observe the emotions expressed in the responses in order to understand and see the underlying meaning of the words.
3. Treat any and all resistance as valuable and necessary. Remember, resistance is part of the process and allows new information to become acceptable.
4. Create or negotiate an aligned goal that satisfies the interests of all parties involved.
5. Balance the need for long-term goals with short-term outcomes. You have heard the saying, "Don't sweat the small stuff."
6. Generate new ideas and innovative solutions.

As you move through this process, ask yourself these questions:

- Do I need to do anything differently to be effective as a leader?
- What is the most critical situation I need to resolve with a direct report, business partner, or my manager to achieve my business goals?
- What actions do I need to take to resolve this situation?

Growing Employees: Making the Difference

To sustain growth and retain valued employees, Top Performance Leaders need to create a context, or environment, for developing future leaders—an environment where employees are encouraged to grow and deliver results that are aligned with the organization's vision. Remember, an environment is the emotional, physical, intellectual, and spiritual "space" of an organization. As a leader, you create the environment: through the way you speak to people, the way you handle your work, and the way you take care of the everyday activities of your organization.

Creating an effective workplace environment

Consciously or unconsciously, we are always creating an environment. Answering the following questions will help you assess your workplace environment. Your answers may help you decide who in your organization needs coaching and how you may want to do it.

- Do you say what you think? Or do you attempt to wash over what is happening? Do people you deal with know what you think and feel?
- What is your role in creating an environment?
- What is the environment that you want to create with your direct reports, team members, business partners, or manager? Do you want an open, honest, productive, and trusting space? What is your preference?
- As a leader, do you create the required environment to achieve the results you want?
- How do you do it?
- Do you influence? How?
- Do others accept you as a leader? How?
- Do you feel encouraged and supported by the direct reports?
- What actions positively affect the environment?
- What actions negatively affect the environment?
- How do you create an overall environment that facilitates your organization's business aims?
- Who is responsible for ensuring success?

Coaching others

Below are coaching guidelines that use the communication skills discussed in this book. These coaching guidelines can be incorporated in any coaching model used in your company. In the leadership development arena there are many excellent coaching models.

Coaching Guidelines

1. What do you see as a coach that calls for improvement or development? What does the coach need to be successful? Does he have the required passion, commitment, and desire? Assess the situation on the basis of what you have learned so far.

2. Collaborate with other coaches on the preceding issues. Discuss, raise questions, and support the person to locate the key issues. Listen, listen, and listen some more

3. Prioritize the issues. Most of an individual's performance comes directly from only 20 percent of his or her behavior. Focusing on this area of behavior yields the best results.

4. Develop an action plan. Define specific, measurable goals while staying open to input.

5. Develop an ongoing follow-up process that includes evaluative measures designed by you and the other coaches.

Support your coachee to:

- Create a clear vision. As explained in a previous chapter, a clear vision is simple and visual (you can picture it in your mind) and addresses future possibilities, not the past.

- Enlist the support of others. Enlisting others in the effort for change is potentially one of the most powerful steps that can be taken. It helps keep the person being coached authentic, honest, and accountable.

- Make a public commitment. Letting others know what you are attempting to do increases the likelihood of success. It creates accountability and encourages others to support the person in his or her efforts.
- Be specific. Specific goals make it easier to assess if one is succeeding or failing, and helps to measure success.

Mentoring others

Mentoring is a partnership where the mentor (who usually has a record of success in a role similar to that of the protégé) shares the responsibility for developing the desired qualities in the protégé, and ultimately leading him or her to success. The mentoring partnership focuses on the long term results. It is closely related to coaching, yet it implies more involvement.

Guidelines for Mentoring

1. Establish a partnership for learning. Set the tone for an ongoing relationship. Create rapport through openness and authenticity.
2. Foster acceptance. Without an environment of acceptance, the protégé will not take the risks involved in the process of change.

3. Listen without an agenda. This is difficult at times when being a mentor as you are in that role because you are the "expert." Be willing to be guided by your protégé. Try to learn what you do not know. Always be willing to listen.

4. Ask permission before giving advice or feedback. Asking permission puts the protégé in a position of responsibility and creates accountability. If the protégé does not really want the advice or feedback, it can be ignored. In the initial stages of the partnership, let it be agreed upon that you will ask and they will respond honestly before giving or receiving advice or feedback.

5. Give advice and feedback. Giving advice can provide information to the person being mentored about something he or she may be aware of and yet does not understand fully. Giving feedback is giving your perception of a person's response to a situation, and may not be something the protégé is aware of. Oftentimes mentors give feedback to the protégé about areas that are "blind spots." The intention is to direct the protégé's attention to the blind spot so that ultimately he or she can see it clearly without external help.

AFTERWORD

This book is a testament to authenticity and self-awareness. As a Top Performing Leader, you have earned the right to be authentic. Once you are able to communicate and connect in an emotionally intelligent, responsible manner, you will notice that colleagues in your sphere of influence are moving closer to you. They will automatically align with your vision. You will have enough space around you to accommodate them and their individual goals. Your way of thinking will create a culture of motivation as you do your work as a leader. Once you stand behind your words, your actions and thoughts will be in mutual agreement. You will be congruent. As you experience yourself as a Top Performance Leader, you will see the world from a place of awareness and paradox will be natural; uncertainty will allow you and the people around you to grow and continue to learn.

Our business environment now is a dynamic, forever changing melody of technological changes and emerging opportunities. Whereas in the past, bricks and mortar defined the "where" of the company and seniority defined the "who" of leadership, today web-based clusters of virtual teams and meritocracies define emerging leaders. The complexities of science and multinational and globally distributed sites make Top Performance

Leadership equivalent to self-awareness and authenticity.

In an environment of "experience economy," a term coined by Jim Collins, leadership needs to be intelligence-oriented and awareness-focused. Rather than attempting to control and contain conflict, such leaders know that new solutions arise from the paradox-holding of their peers and from direct reports. Leaders need to spend time with this paradox and allow their team to think as well as act.

INDEX

D

M

N

O

P

ABOUT THE AUTHOR

Judith Orloff, MEd, is a coach, master facilitator, trainer of trainers, and strategic program designer and senior executive with thirty years of experience in the area of helping people learn. She is president of Orloff Learning, Inc., a company based in Boulder, Colorado, that focuses on helping people create more meaning in their life, and Real Impact Learning, an organization that designs and develops Leadership Development based on Emotional Mastery and Cultural Intelligence. Orloff has been an instructor in the Urban Studies department at the University of Pennsylvania, she co-founded Burlington College in Burlington, Vermont, and developed its BA and MA programs in Transpersonal Psychology, and she taught at the University of Vermont in the College of Education where she received her Masters of Education. She spent over ten years as a psychotherapist and workshop facilitator in the United States, Australia, and New Zealand. She was also the president and CEO of Educational Discoveries, a strategic learning company.

She has worked extensively with the leadership of Bank of America, Fleet Bank, Midas International, Caterpillar, Cargill, General Motors, Ford Thailand, WellBridge, Lubuvitch of Bucks County, Bonai Shalom in Boulder, and many others. Orloff is the author of *The Top Performer's Guide to Leadership* (Sourcebooks, 2008).